Borealis

A Polar Bear Cub's First Year

WALRUS
B O O K S

Story by Rebecca L. Grambo   Photography by Daniel J. Cox

The icy waters of Hudson Bay splash against the Canadian coastline. Plentiful food and a chance to start hunting seals earlier in the winter make the land and water around Churchill, Manitoba a good place for polar bears. About a thousand bears spend their whole lives here, right from the day they are born in dens along the coast to the south. Female polar bears who are going to have cubs make dens in the hills along the river and among the trees. Snowdrifts form over them as the weather grows colder. Here, hidden away in the icy darkness of the northern winter, the story of Borealis (boh-ree-AL-iss) began.

The blizzard winds of early January howled across the land. Less than a day old, a tiny, fuzzy white polar bear cub snuggled into his mother's warm fur. He weighed about half a kilogram (just over a pound) and his eyes were still closed. But tucked safely inside the snug den, little Borealis drank his Mama's rich milk. He grew bigger and stronger every day.

NEWFOUNDLAND

PRINCE EDWARD
ISLAND

NOVA
SCOTIA

The snow over the den broke apart as Mama poked her head through the wall of the den. She lifted her nose and sniffed carefully to make sure there were no predators nearby. It was March and time for Borealis to see the outside world. Mama climbed out of the den and slowly stretched as she looked around.

"Come out, Borealis," Mama invited. A small black nose appeared at the den opening.

After the dark, warm, quiet den, Borealis did not know if he liked the outside. "It's cold, Mama," he cried. The bright sunlight made him squint. "What are all those sounds, Mama? I'm afraid!"

"Sssh, Borealis. It's okay." Mama understood. They spent the next week close to the den so that Borealis could get used to this strange new world. Mama nursed her little one often and snuggled him to keep him warm.

"I'm very hungry, Borealis," Mama said one day. "I haven't eaten since I went into the den. That's more than six months ago! Since then I've been living on the fat stored in my body. And I've been feeding you, little one. Although you're not so little anymore. You must weigh more than ten times as much as when you were born."

"Where can we find some food?" wondered Borealis.

"Follow me!" Mama called. "We will go out on the sea ice where I can hunt for a nice fat seal. I'll walk slowly so that you can keep up."

"How do we catch a seal, Mama?" Borealis asked when they reached the ice.

"First, I look and smell to find the holes in the ice where the seals come up for air. Let's see if we can find one." After some time, Mama found a breathing hole. She led Borealis away from it and told him to stay put until she called him. Mama walked slowly back to the hole and crouched beside it. She stayed very still. Borealis stayed still, too. They waited and waited. Finally, Borealis heard a tiny noise and suddenly there was a seal in the hole! Mama grabbed the seal in her jaws and dragged it out onto the ice.

"Come, Borealis!" she called.

He raced over to the seal. Mama ate the fat, or blubber, while Borealis chewed on the meat. It was tough for his small teeth, but he kept trying.

"Now I feel better," Mama said after the meal. "Come and let me wash your face, little one." With her black tongue she gently licked the cub's face. "Time for a nap. You crawl up onto my back, Borealis. Until you get a nice thick fat layer to keep you warm, you'll get too cold sleeping on the ice."

Borealis snuggled into Mama's soft fur. Warm and with full tummies, the two bears fell asleep and dreamed of seals.

Borealis and his mother had good luck finding seals. Mama caught more of the animals at their breathing holes. And this was the time of year when seals gave birth to their pups. Mama could smell the seals from a kilometre and a half (over a mile) away, even though their dens were under a layer of ice and snow. When she found a den, Mama smashed through the roof and snatched the fat seal pup inside.

"I'm glad you catch so many seals," Borealis said one day as they were eating.

"Yes," Mama agreed. "It's important that we get enough to eat before the ice melts and I can't hunt seals anymore. And other animals depend on us, too. The arctic foxes and ravens eat all the scraps we leave behind."

"Is that why foxes have been following us?" Borealis asked. He had often wondered why the tiny little foxes dared to come so close to Mama.

"That's right," said Mama. "They clean up our leftovers and that is enough food to keep them alive. You'll see foxes far out on the ice next winter, following polar bears to share their meals."

The weather slowly grew warmer. The ice began to melt and break up. Sometimes the bears had to swim from one patch of ice to the next. Mama's fat layer kept her warm as she dog-paddled slowly through the cold water. Borealis rode on her back to keep from getting chilled.

As the big pieces of ice grew smaller, seals became harder to find. One evening Mama looked around. She lifted her head and sniffed at the breeze. "Summer is coming, Borealis. It's time for us to head back to land. We'll stay on shore until it freezes up again next winter."

They headed off to see what the summer would bring.

"Wow, there are birds everywhere," Borealis said in wonder. He watched them cross the sky and listened to their voices. The first birds had come in late April. Many more had followed.

"Some of them keep on flying even farther north to raise their families," Mama told him. "But others bring up their babies right here. See that white lump way over there? In the middle of that patch of bare ground?"

Borealis looked at the lump. He thought it was a rock. Suddenly two big yellow eyes opened and glared at him.

"That's a snowy owl on her nest," Mama said. "If there are a lot of hares or lemmings around for food, the owl raises a bigger family than if food is hard to find. The chicks …"

"What are lemmings?" Borealis cut in.

"Don't interrupt, Borealis. Lemmings are small rodents, something like mice," Mama said. "The owl chicks leave the nest when they're only about a month old, but they stay close by so their parents can feed them.The summer is almost over by the time they're able to fly."

"May I go look at the nest?" Borealis asked.

"No, Borealis. Mother snowy owls do not like anyone to come near their nest. She would get mad and attack you." Mama turned and walked away.

Borealis started to argue. Then he thought about the owl's sharp talons and the look in those big yellow eyes. He shook his head and ran to catch up with Mama.

"There is too much sunshine," a hot, grumpy Borealis complained. He had noticed the sun staying in the sky a little longer each day since they had left the den. "Pretty soon it will be light all the time and I'll melt!"

"Don't worry," Mama said. "The longest day of the year is just a few days away. After that, every night lasts a little longer until the middle of winter. Then night starts to shrink and the days grow longer again."

"Why do the days change like that?" asked Borealis.

"I don't know. A bear I knew once heard some people talk about Earth being tilted, with the top tipped toward the sun for half the year and away for the other half. Maybe light and dark agreed long ago to share the seasons this way. It has been the same for as long as bears remember."

Borealis knew what people were. Mama had shown him some one day. She kept talking. "Plants living here grow quickly in the long days. That's important because our summer only lasts about two months. In that short time, a plant must grow big enough to bloom and make the seed that will turn into next summer's plants. Watch and see, Borealis."

Mama was right. Each day, new patches of bright flowers appeared and soon the tundra was filled with color.

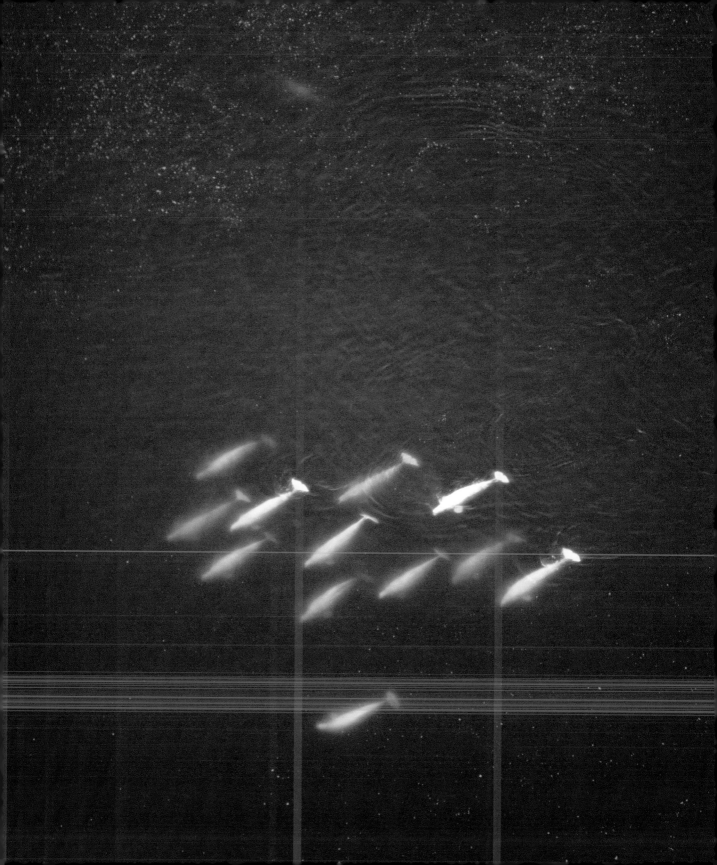

Borealis and Mama spent most of the summer near the water, taking a swim now and then to cool off. There were no seals to eat. Although she sometimes nibbled on things they found along the shore, Mama ate almost nothing. She would have to wait until the ice came again before her next real meal. Borealis didn't go hungry, though. Mama was still able to nurse him.

One day, Borealis saw a misty spout of water shoot up from the waves — and then another and another!

"Mama, what's that?" he asked excitedly.

"Those are beluga whales breathing," she explained. "They are small, white whales about twice as long as me. North of us, thousands of belugas gather each summer to have their babies and to eat fish. The birds say that, from overhead, the blue water looks polka-dotted with groups of whales."

Borealis lay in the shade next to Mama. "Summer means birds and flowers and belugas," he thought sleepily.

The bright tundra flowers disappeared. Leaves and grasses changed from green to red and gold. And it was definitely getting colder. Summer was over and Borealis thought it might snow any day.

Some of the animals around him were changing, too, Borealis noticed. He spied some ptarmigan (TAR-mih-gun) among the willows. The brown birds now wore patches of white feathers. "Ptarmigan turn white every fall so that they blend in with the snow," Mama told him. "That's called camouflage (CAM-oh-flahj). It helps to hide them from predators. Their brown feathers do the same job in the summer."

"Do other animals change color in the fall?" Borealis wondered.

"Yes," Mama answered. "Arctic foxes and arctic hares both turn white in the fall and brown again in the spring."

"Why don't we change color, Mama?" Borealis asked.

"I don't know," Mama replied. "Maybe because we only need to blend in when we are hunting seals on the ice."

"Mama," Borealis asked as they rested together later, "do you ever get tired of me asking questions?"

"No, Borealis. That is how little bears learn about things, by watching and listening to their mothers."

The cold snow felt so good! The first few snows had quickly melted, but finally some stayed around. Borealis, who had been very hot all summer in his fur, loved to slide on his tummy and roll in the snow.

"Come on, Mama!" he cried. "Let's play!" He lay on his back and wiggled his paws in the air.

"I'm going to get you," she laughed. She stood up on her hind legs, then pounced on him.

The two bears, one big and one little, rolled over and over until they had to stop for a rest.

That night, the sky was clear and millions of stars sparkled overhead. During the night, Borealis rolled over and sleepily opened his eyes. All of a sudden he was wide awake.

"Mama!" Borealis cried. "Wake up!"

"What's wrong?" Mama asked.

"Look at the sky, Mama. It's moving!"

Mama looked around and gave a low chuckle. Shimmering curtains of greenish–yellow light were sweeping across the sky. Some of them seemed to almost touch the ground.

"It's okay, Borealis," Mama reassured him. "Those are the Northern Lights. They won't hurt you."

"What are they?" Borealis asked, still frightened.

"Well," Mama answered, "I have heard people looking at the lights say that energy from the sun heats gases high up in the sky. It makes them glow. But long ago bears heard the people who lived here then say that the lights were the spirits of their ancestors playing football in the sky."

"They are pretty," Borealis decided, "whatever they are."

"Yes," Mama agreed, "and you are named after them. Their other name is Aurora Borealis. Aurora means light and Borealis means northern."

"Cool!" said the little bear. He fell asleep watching the flickering sky.

In the area around Churchill, Mama and Borealis began to meet more and more polar bears. One morning, Borealis saw a young bear doing something strange. It stood very still in the snow and then pounced forward with its front paws.

"What's he doing, Mama?" Borealis wondered.

"I bet he's playing with a lemming," Mama replied. "Look! There's one over there!"

Borealis spied a gray, mouse-sized animal near the edge of the snow. "I can get it!" he cried and plunged forward into the snow.

But the lemming was gone. All Borealis got was a nose full of snow.

"Phew!" he sneezed. "Where did it go?"

"Lemmings have all kinds of tunnels under the snow," Mama told him. "They keep busy all winter finding seeds and other things to eat."

"Do they taste good?" Borealis asked.

"We don't usually eat them," Mama answered as she turned to go. "They are very little and hard to catch. It uses up more energy to catch one than you get from eating it. Owls and foxes eat lemmings, though. Some years there are lots of lemmings. Then the owls and foxes have big families. In other years, there are very few lemmings. The owls and foxes can't get enough to eat and many of them die."

The two bears walked away, headed for the shore of Hudson Bay. From a tiny hole in the snow, a pair of eyes set in a gray, furry face watched them go.

Borealis turned his head as a movement in the nearby willows caught his eye. Two cubs lay cuddled up in the snow with their mother. They watched curiously as Borealis and Mama passed by. Then the two cubs closed their eyes and went back to sleep.

In the past few days, Borealis had seen many mothers with their cubs. There were lots of other bears here, too. Borealis had never guessed that there were so many polar bears. Usually polar bears stayed away from each other. What was going on?

"Mama, how come we're here? And why are all these other bears here?" Borealis wanted to know.

"Polar bears have come here at the beginning of winter for a very long time," Mama told him. "The sea freezes here before it freezes at other places around the bay. Each year, the first sea ice strong enough for us to walk on forms near the place people call Cape Churchill. That's the little, skinny piece of land that we went to yesterday. I wanted to see if the ice was getting any thicker."

"The sooner we can get out on the ice, the sooner we can catch seals. Right, Mama?" Now Borealis understood why everyone was here. After a long summer of going without food and living on their stored fat, the polar bears were hungry. So they came to Churchill and waited for the ice.

Borealis yawned and looked around. He and Mama had spent most of the last few days resting and sleeping. That is what the other bears seemed to be doing, too. Mama told him that they were saving as much energy as possible until they could finally get some real food. For now, all there seemed to be to eat was some kelp, a kind of seaweed. Borealis did not like kelp very much.

Borealis sat up. Not all the bears were sleeping. Two males stood on their hind legs pushing and shoving each other. They did not look like they were really trying to hurt each other. Borealis had seen other bears wrestling like this, too. Sometimes they just rolled around in the snow.

"What are those bears doing, Mama?"

She opened her eyes and lifted her head to look. "They are sparring with each other, Borealis. Male bears do that this time of year."

"Do they hurt each other?" Borealis asked.

"Not usually, although sometimes one of them gets a little rough and scratches or cuts the other one. See how they only spar with someone about their own size? That makes it safer. Later on in the year, when they are fighting over a female, male bears fight for real. One of them often gets hurt. Here it seems to be more like play. You will get to spar in a few years, Borealis. Then you'll know all about it."

Borealis rolled onto his tummy and rested his head on his paws. He watched the big bears smack and shove each other. He wondered what it would be like to be one of them.

Borealis moved closer to his mother as the thing came toward them. He had seen these things before. They crawled over the land like big, loud bugs. But they did not have legs, just round black feet under their white bodies.

"Mama," Borealis began to whine, "what ..."

"Hush, little one," she told him. "Those things are full of noisy people and smell funny, but they won't hurt you. Every year about this time, all kinds of people ride out here in those machines."

"Are they waiting for the ice, too?" wondered Borealis.

"Maybe," Mama agreed. "They seem to spend a lot of time in the same places we do."

"Can we go closer to look at the people, Mama?" Borealis asked.

"Just a little bit, but don't get too close. People can be unpredictable," Mama cautioned.

The two bears moved closer and watched as other bears went right up to the machine.

"Seen enough?" Mama asked.

"Yes, Mama," Borealis replied. "But we're lucky to see them when they are migrating, aren't we?"

the Tundra Buggy

The weather turned very cold. The people and their big machines were almost all gone. Each day the bears went down to the shore. They looked at the ice and walked on it to see how far out they could go. Foxes checked the ice, too. Everyone was waiting, waiting.

Late one afternoon, a blizzard wind began to blow. It howled through the night as the bears slept snugly tucked in the snow.

"Get up, Borealis," Mama said as she nudged him the next morning. "The ice is thick enough. It's time for us to go."

All around him, Borealis saw bears moving toward the coast. As he and Mama reached the shore, Borealis could see the tiny shapes of bears already far out on the ice.

"Here we go, Borealis, " Mama said. "Are you excited about spending your first winter on the ice?"

"Yeesss," Borealis said, "and a little scared, too, I think. I don't know what's going to happen."

"That's okay, little one." Mama nuzzled him. "I will be with you all the time. And you will be busy watching and learning more things a grown-up bear must know. Just like you have been this summer. Ready?"

"Yes, Mama." Borealis felt better. Mama always took care of him and there would be things to see. And things to ask questions about!

So off they went, a big bear and a little bear heading for new adventures.

Here is a bit more information about some of the things in this story:

POLAR BEARS

➢ There are about 22,000 polar bears in the world.

➢ 60% of them live in Canada; the rest in Russia, Greenland/Denmark, Norway, and the United States.

➢ Polar bears are one of the world's largest predators. Males are about 900–1300 lbs (400–600 kg), 6.5–8 ft (2–2.5 m) long; females 550–650 lbs (250–300 kg), 6–6.5 ft (1.8–2 m) long.

➢ A male's paw may be 1 ft (30 cm) wide.

➢ Polar bears mate in spring but female doesn't really become pregnant until autumn, and only if she's fat and healthy enough. She must be able to feed herself and her cubs from stored fat until she is able to hunt again the following spring.

➢ Females usually give birth to one or two cubs, each about 1 ft (30 cm) long, weighing just over 1 lb (454 grams). Cubs stay with their mother for up to two and a half years, learning hunting skills.

➢ Polar bears that live in places like Churchill, where the ice melts in summer, become stranded on shore. They fast, or go without food, until the ice freezes and they can hunt again. A black bear would die if it couldn't eat for this long, but a polar bear's body slows down to use less energy.

➢ Polar bears live to be 15 to 18 years old in the wild, although a few over 30 have been found.

➢ An adult polar bear's only enemies are human hunters and, sometimes, other bears.

Get more information about polar bears:
Polar Bear International's website: http://www.polarbearsalive.org/

BELUGAS

➢ Belugas are very small compared to some whales, about 13 ft (4 m) long.

➢ Their calves are born brownish-red but soon turn to a deep bluish-gray, then gradually get lighter. They are creamy white when they are about 6 years old.

➢ Constantly chirping and trilling, belugas are one of the noisiest whales. They use the sounds they make to find food, to talk to one another, and to find their way when they swim under the ice.

CHANGING DAY LENGTH

➢ Earth doesn't stand up straight. As it moves around the sun, the amount of sunlight that the northern and southern halves receive changes.

➢ During summer in the Northern Hemisphere, the North Pole points toward the sun and we have long, warm days. June 21 is the longest day of the year. Then days grow shorter as Earth moves to a position where the North Pole points away from the sun.

➢ The shortest day of the year in the Northern Hemisphere is December 21. After that, our days grow longer and then the whole cycle begins again.

➢ In the Southern Hemisphere, seasons are reversed. They have summer while we have winter.

CHURCHILL, MANITOBA

➢ Thousands of people visit each year to see polar bears. Some come in summer to see birds, flowers, and belugas, too. Most come in autumn to watch the bears as they wait for the ice.

➢ Visitors travel onto the tundra in special vehicles that can cope with the boggy landscape. The number of vehicles and what their passengers can do is strictly controlled to make sure no harm comes to the bears.

INDEX

Text copyright © 2003 by Rebecca L. Grambo · Photographs copyright © 2003 by Daniel J. Cox
Second printing, 2009
Walrus Books, an imprint of Whitecap books

Edited by Elizabeth McLean · Cover and interior design by Robert A. Yerks/visualanguage llc.

Printed and bound in China

Library and Archives Canada Cataloguing in Publication

Grambo, Rebecca, 1963–

Borealis: a polar bear cub's first year / Rebecca L. Grambo; Daniel J. Cox, photographer.

(Wild beginnings; 1)

ISBN 10: 1-55285-465-5
ISBN 13: 978-1-55285-465-5

1. Polar bear–Juvenile literature. I. Cox, Daniel J., 1960– II. Title. III. Series: Wild beginnings (North Vancouver, B.C.)

QL737.C27G71 2003   j599.786   C2003-911230-6

The publisher acknowledges the financial support of the Canada Council for the Arts, the British Columbia Arts Council, and the Government of Canada through the Book Publishing Industry Development Program (BPIDP). Whitecap Books also acknowledges the financial support of the Province of British Columbia through the Book Publishing Tax Credit.

Canada Council for the Arts Conseil des Arts du Canada

BRITISH COLUMBIA ARTS COUNCIL